Math Tutor: Mastering Multiplication and Division

By
HAL TORRANCE

COPYRIGHT © 2004 Mark Twain Media, Inc.

ISBN 1-58037-256-2

Printing No. CD-1616

Mark Twain Media, Inc., Publishers
Distributed by Carson-Dellosa Publishing Company, Inc.

Table of Contents

How to Use This Book

Each new concept is introduced in a short ABSORB! section. The absorb section primarily focuses on a single skill or concept. Key terms are highlighted for easy identification. The APPLY! section then gives the student practice in that skill.

It is advised not to skip ahead to miscellaneous topics. This is due to the sequential nature of mathematics and the systematic way in which this book has been arranged. For instance, recognizing the factors of a number is an underlying skill for division. So a review of factors is presented prior to most of the division material.

The section **Final Review: All Topics** will serve as a good pretest if one is needed for planning a more focused course of study. There are also two **Section Reviews** that focus on cumulative skills presented to that point in the book.

What follows are descriptions and suggested uses for each section of this book:

1. **What Are Multiplication and Division? (3 pgs.)** reviews the concepts of multiplication and division. Models are used for demonstrating the way in which multiplication is linked to addition and the way in which division is linked to subtraction.

2. **Math Facts: Multiplication Tables and Multiples (2 pgs.)** reviews the concepts of a multiple and basic multiplication math facts. *Note:* If there is lack of student mastery of the multiplication tables, then parallel study in this area is advised. Most of the problems contained in this book rely on having a working mastery of the multiplication tables of at least 1 x 1 through 9 x 9.

3. **Multiplying by a Single-Digit Number (2 pgs.)** reviews the process for single-digit multiplication.

4. **The Easy Process of Multiplying by 10 (1 pg.)** reviews the special circumstances involved in multiplication by 10.

5. **Multiplying by Two-Digit Numbers (2 pgs.)** reviews the process for multiplying by two-digit numbers.

6. **Multiplying by Three-Digit Numbers (2 pgs.)** reviews the process for multiplying by three-digit numbers.

7. **Multiplying by 100, 1,000, or More (1 pg.)** reviews the technique of solving by inspection problems that involve powers of 10.

How to Use This Book (cont.)

Section Review 1 (2 pgs.) provides practice problems for reviewing all sections covered to this point.

8. **Dividing by Single-Digit Numbers (3 pgs.)** reviews division by single-digit numbers with both models and standard division format.

9. **Understanding Factors: Dividing Made Easier (2 pgs.)** reviews factors and the way in which factoring relates to the division process.

10. **Dividing by 10 (1 pg.)** builds on previous work multiplying by 10 to demonstrate division as an inverse operation.

11. **What is r? (2 pgs.)** reviews the meaning of the term "remainder" and how to express the remainder as a fraction.

12. **Dividing by Two-Digit Numbers (3 pgs.)** reviews the process for dividing by two-digit numbers.

13. **Dividing by Three-Digit Numbers (2 pgs.)** reviews the process for dividing by three-digit numbers.

    Section Review 2 (2 pgs.) provides practice problems for reviewing all sections covered to this point.

14. **A Quick Look at Decimal Numbers (2 pgs.)** builds on previous work writing the remainder as a fraction and demonstrates multiplication and division of decimals as a calculator activity. A calculator is recommended for this activity.

15. **Multiplying With Decimal Numbers (2 pgs.)** reviews the rules for multiplying with decimals and provides mixed practice.

16. **Dividing With Decimal Numbers (2 pgs.)** reviews the rules for dividing by decimals and provides mixed practice.

17. **Estimating the Result of Multiplication and Division (2 pgs.)** reviews the techniques for estimating products and quotients.

    Final Review: All Sections (3 pgs.) provides practice problems for reviewing all sections. It may also be used as a pretest to plan a more focused course of study.

What Are Multiplication and Division? 1

 We know that multiplication is related to addition. When a number is multiplied, it is basically being added over and over again. Consider the following.

$$8 \times 4 = 32$$

and likewise

$$8 + 8 + 8 + 8 = 32$$

This simple example illustrates the way in which addition and multiplication are related. You can see that multiplication makes this process of combining numbers easier since it allows for fewer steps in the process.

In this same way, division is related to subtraction. Dividing a number is basically the same as taking away a piece of that number each time. Consider the following.

$$20 \div 4 = 5$$

So 20 can subtract 5 exactly 4 times.

$$20 - 5 - 5 - 5 - 5 = 0$$

It can be said in a general sense that multiplication and division are opposites, just as addition and subtraction are opposites. Multiplication causes an increase, while division causes a decrease in the size of the number involved.

Consider the following model, a group of triangles that have been arranged.

With your pencil's point, count the triangles in this group. (You should get a total of 40.)

Name: _____ **Date:** _____

What Are Multiplication and Division? (cont.) 1

If you happened to notice that the triangles were arranged in rows with 5 triangles across, you could simply have multiplied the number of rows by the number of triangles in each row (8 x 5 = 40).

Now consider this: Into how many groups of 4 triangles can this model be split? With a pencil, draw circles around groups of 4 triangles.

You should have been able to draw 10 groups of 4 triangles. This is the nature of division (40 ÷ 4 = 10).

For each of the groups shown, use multiplication of rows and columns to determine how many figures each model is composed of. (Concentrate on multiplication for now, since we'll work with division models later in the book.)

1. Rows _____   Columns _____   Total Figures _____

2. Rows _____   Columns _____   Total Figures _____

3. Rows _____   Columns _____   Total Figures _____

4

Name: _____ **Date:** _____

What Are Multiplication and Division? (cont.) 1

4. Rows _____ Columns _____ Total Figures _____

● ● ● ● ● ● ● ● ● ● ● ●
● ● ● ● ● ● ● ● ● ● ● ●

5. Rows _____ Columns _____ Total Figures _____

✳ ✳ ✳ ✳
✳ ✳ ✳ ✳
✳ ✳ ✳ ✳
✳ ✳ ✳ ✳
✳ ✳ ✳ ✳
✳ ✳ ✳ ✳
✳ ✳ ✳ ✳
✳ ✳ ✳ ✳
✳ ✳ ✳ ✳

6. Now draw your own model to show the number 36.

Rows _____ Columns _____ Total Figures _____

Name: _____ **Date:** _____

Math Facts: Multiplication Tables and Multiples 2

 Consider the following problem.

$$\begin{array}{r} 334{,}566 \\ \times \quad 289 \\ \hline \end{array}$$

We're not going to solve this problem just now, but recognize that these large numbers are all made up of single digits. To solve this multiplication problem involves working with each of those digits, one at a time. This is where knowledge of math facts, in this case the multiplication tables, becomes important.

In the Apply section, we'll work a bit with math fact problems. For the moment, let's turn our attention to a basic term, **multiple.** Consider the following.

> 35 is a multiple of 5 because 5 x 7 = 35
> 18 is a multiple of 3 because 3 x 6 = 18
> 48 is a multiple of 8 because 8 x 6 = 48

Using what we know about multiples, we could list the multiples of a number such as 4.

> 4 : 4,   8,   12 ,   16,   20   the list of multiples for 4 continues ...
>   (4 x 1) (4 x 2) (4 x 3) (4 x 4) (4 x 5)

You can see from this example that a multiplication table is really no more than a list of the multiples for each number.

For each of the numbers given, write a list of its next 11 multiples.

1. 6 _____

2. 4 _____

3. 10 _____

4. 7 _____

Name: _____ **Date:** _____

Math Facts: Multiplication Tables and Multiples (cont.) 2

Answer the following math fact problems as quickly as you are able. If you are stumped by a problem, skip over it and return once you've gotten to the bottom of the list. If you are still stumped by a problem, make a model using rows and columns of dots in order to solve it.

5. 2 x 9 = _____

6. 11 x 9 = _____

7. 3 x 7 = _____

8. 10 x 11 = _____

9. 5 x 6 = _____

10. 8 x 5 = _____

11. 8 x 4 = _____

12. 6 x 6 = _____

13. 1 x 12 = _____

14. 11 x 5 = _____

15. 4 x 4 = _____

16. 12 x 2 = _____

17. 5 x 9 = _____

18. 6 x 5 = _____

19. 6 x 7 = _____

20. 1 x 9 = _____

21. 4 x 11 = _____

22. 8 x 7 = _____

23. 3 x 9 = _____

24. 4 x 7 = _____

25. 9 x 9 = _____

26. 11 x 7 = _____

27. 8 x 2 = _____

28. 9 x 6 = _____

29. 10 x 6 = _____

30. 11 x 12 = _____

Multiplying by a Single-Digit Number 3

Multiplication by a single-digit number is perhaps the easiest kind of problem type other than those found in the multiplication tables. Consider the following problem.

	step 1	**step 2**	**step 3**
324	324	324	324
x 2	x 2	x 2	x 2
?	8	48	648

In this problem, the 2 was multiplied by each digit in turn. None of the numbers created **"carry-overs,"** or instances where a number greater than nine was the result of the multiplication. In those kinds of problems, numbers must be carried, since the multiplied digit is bigger than the place value.

For instance, 2 x 7 = 14. There isn't a way to write 14 as a single digit, is there? So in a multiplication problem, the "1" would be carried over and added to the result of the next multiplication. Consider the following example:

	step 1	**step 2**	**step 3**
		2	2
192	192	192	192
x 3	x 3	x 3	x 3
?	6	76	576

Tip: In working with multiplication problems, properly setting up the problem can be the difference between finding a correct answer and making a mistake. Always take the extra time to set your problem up in neat columns when writing it out on a piece of paper. Numbers that are to be carried should be neatly written atop the column to which they apply. Stray or sloppy numbers equal mistakes!

Also, when you see a problem written out like this: 445 x 8, convert it to this:

445
x 8

This vertical format makes the problem easier to solve.

8

Name: _____ **Date:** _____

Multiplying by a Single-Digit Number (cont.) 3

APPLY!

Solve.

1. 223	2. 114	3. 323
x 3	x 2	x 3

4. 419	5. 676	6. 912
x 4	x 5	x 2

7. 927	8. 299	9. 771
x 4	x 6	x 9

10. 515	11. 249	12. 634
x 7	x 3	x 4

13. 999	14. 101	15. 844
x 9	x 7	x 5

16. 398 x 8 = _____

17. 708 x 4 = _____

Name: _____ Date: _____

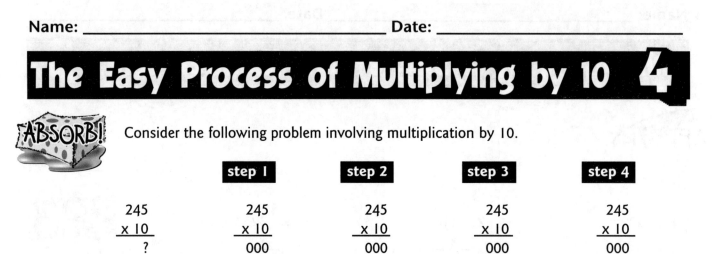

The Easy Process of Multiplying by 10 4

Consider the following problem involving multiplication by 10.

	step 1	**step 2**	**step 3**	**step 4**
245	245	245	245	245
x 10	x 10	x 10	x 10	x 10
?	000	000	000	000
		2450	+ 2450	+ 2450
			?	2,450

Multiplying a number by a two-digit number ordinarily involves multiplying each digit by each digit in turn. But multiplying a number by 10 is a special circumstance. Those kinds of problems can be readily solved by inspection.

If the answer in the problem above looks familiar, it's because the answer is basically the number we began with, except a zero has been added to the end of it, 2450. Multiplying a number by 10 essentially moves the number over one place value. 245 became 2,450. Likewise, 500 x 10 would be 5,000. And 25 x 10 is 250.

APPLY!

Solve each problem using inspection.

1. 75	2. 145	3. 900	4. 2,240
x 10	x 10	x 10	x 10

5. 313	6. 555	7. 1,000	8. 102
x 10	x 10	x 10	x 10

9. 12,005 x 10 = _____   10. 850 x 10 = _____

Multiplying by Two-Digit Numbers **5**

 In the previous section, we already reviewed the process of multiplying by a two-digit number, 10. The process used for multiplying any two-digit number is quite the same, though multiplying by 10 gives us an especially easy result due to its special circumstances. Consider the following example.

step 1	step 2	step 3	step 4	step 5
144	144	144	144	144
x 21	x 21	x 21	x 21	x 21
?	4	44	144	144
			0	80

step 6	step 7	step 8	step 9
144	144	144	144
x 21	x 21	x 21	x 21
144	144	144	144
880	2880	+ 2880	+ 2880
			3,024

Tip: Whew! It looks like a lot of steps, and this problem had no carry-overs. But consider for a moment that the process itself is not something you always have to think about step by step. For instance, does a running horse have to think about bending each leg and moving each leg as it runs? Of course not! Likewise, once you are familiar with the process itself, you don't have to rehearse in your mind that there are 9 steps for solving a two-digit multiplication problem.

Name: _____ **Date:** _____

Multiplying by Two-Digit Numbers (cont.) 5

 APPLY!

Solve. Remember to write any carry-overs atop the column to which they apply. Stray numbers equal mistakes!

1.	231 x 23	**2.** 404 x 11	**3.** 122 x 42
4.	818 x 10	**5.** 665 x 78	**6.** 799 x 34
7.	1,200 x 14	**8.** 7,625 x 51	**9.** 10,500 x 11

Rewrite these as vertical problems, and then solve.

10. 8,445 x 10 = _____ **11.** 255 x 99 = _____ **12.** 34,998 x 64 = _____

Name: _____ **Date:** _____

Multiplying by Three-Digit Numbers 6

Multiplying by a three-digit number represents the same process as with two digits, only an extra row of numbers will be created for the final addition step. Consider the following example. A few steps have been eliminated, since we have previously reviewed multiplying by a two-digit number.

	step 7	**step 8**	**step 9**	**step 10**
721	721	721	721	721
x 215	x 215	x 215	x 215	x 215
?	3605	3605	3605	3605
	7210	7210	7210	7210
		00	200	4200

	step 11	**step 12**	**step 13**
	721	721	721
	x 215	x 215	x 215
	3605	3605	3605
	7210	7210	7210
	144200	+ 144200	+ 144200
			155,015

This will probably look a lot like a repeat of the process for multiplying with a two-digit number. Basically it is. The process continues in a like manner whether it is multiplication by a three-digit number or a 13-digit number, for that matter. Each new digit just adds another layer of steps.

Solve.

1.   212
    x 134

2.   133
    x 117

3.   405
    x 555

Name: _____ **Date:** _____

Multiplying by Three-Digit Numbers (cont.) 6

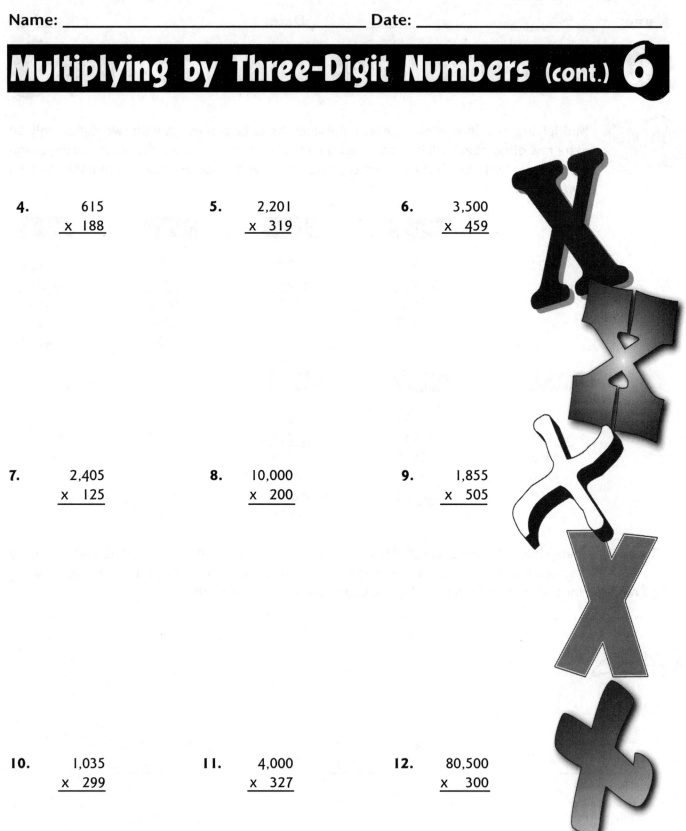

4. 615
    x 188

5. 2,201
    x 319

6. 3,500
    x 459

7. 2,405
    x 125

8. 10,000
    x 200

9. 1,855
    x 505

10. 1,035
    x 299

11. 4,000
    x 327

12. 80,500
    x 300

Name: _____ **Date:** _____

Multiplying by 100, 1,000, or More 7

In a previous section, we learned there was a "trick" of sorts, for multiplying numbers by 10. This same technique works for multiplying numbers by 100, 1,000, and so forth. Consider the following.

$$10 \times 225 = 2,250$$

$$100 \times 225 = 22,500$$

$$1,000 \times 225 = 225,000$$

You may have noticed that a pattern emerged for multiplying numbers by 10, 100, and 1,000. The original number is changed to reflect the number of zeros in the multiplier. When a number is multiplied by 100, it is expanded by 2 decimal places, and therefore 2 zeros are added to the end. 225 became 22,500. Likewise, 1,000 x 225 became 225,000. This pattern of "adding zeros" continues for larger numbers such as 10,000 or 100,000 and beyond.

Solve each problem by inspection.

1. $100 \times 75 =$ _____

2. $10 \times 34 =$ _____

3. $100 \times 255 =$ _____

4. $100 \times 515 =$ _____

5. $1,000 \times 885 =$ _____

6. $1,000 \times 1,542 =$ _____

7. $451 \times 1,000 =$ _____

8. $10,000 \times 65 =$ _____

9. $10,000 \times 375 =$ _____

10. $10,000 \times 1,000 =$ _____

Name: _____ **Date:** _____

Section Review 1

For each of the numbers given, supply the first 8 multiples.

1. 3 _____

2. 11 _____

3. 15 _____

4. 25 _____

Solve.

5.   45
         x 9

6.   115
        x 12

7.   425
        x 25

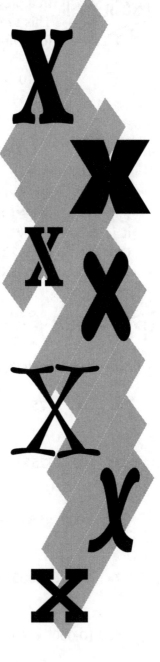

8.   209
         x 7

9.   775
        x 18

10.   1,550
        x   10

11. 335 x 75 = _____

12. 250 x 10 = _____

Name: _____ Date: _____

Section Review 1 (cont.)

13. A car dealer promoted a sale by offering to donate $150 to the local library for each car sold on a particular weekend. The dealer sold 38 cars that weekend. How much money should the car dealer donate to the library to fulfill the promise?

    _____

14. A veterinarian working at a cattle auction gave each animal that passed through the auction four different injections to guard against diseases. A total of 245 animals went through the auction. How many injections did the veterinarian give?

    _____

15. During the harvest at a particular apple farm, each tree produced 125 apples on average. If there were 680 apple trees at this farm, about how many apples were produced?

    _____

16. A truck is carrying 415 crates of potatoes to a processing facility. If each crate of potatoes weighs 44 pounds, how much does the entire cargo of potatoes weigh?

    _____

17. $\begin{array}{r} 929 \\ \times\ 100 \\ \hline \end{array}$

18. $\begin{array}{r} 1{,}205 \\ \times\ 322 \\ \hline \end{array}$

19. $\begin{array}{r} 800 \\ \times\ 299 \\ \hline \end{array}$

20. 15,000 x 125 = _____

21. 200 x 1,000 = _____

22. 65,500 x 120 = _____

Dividing by Single-Digit Numbers 8

 In earlier sections, we worked a bit with multiplication models. We'll make use of models again to demonstrate how division works. Consider the following model.

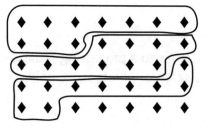

This model can be used to demonstrate division, since 36 ÷ 6 = 6. Another way of looking at it is that 6 groups of 6 each combine to make 36. This example also demonstrates the opposite nature of division and multiplication.

Now consider the next model, based on the problem 35 ÷ 10 = ?

Once 35 has been divided into groups of 10, there are 3 groups of ten, with 5 left over (the remainder). In math terms it is written like this:

35 ÷ 10 = 3 r5

These models are fine when the numbers being divided are pretty small, but models begin to lose their practical value as the numbers being divided get larger. What if the number being divided is 500? That's a bit large to take care of with a math model.

We most often see division problems set up in the following way:

250 ÷ 7 = _____   or   7)‾2‾5‾0‾

Both of the forms shown above are standard ways of writing division problems. But as with multiplication, it is easier to work in a vertical format as provided by the form on the right.

Dividing by Single-Digit Numbers (cont.) 8

Example 1: Consider the problem 225 ÷ 9 = ?

	step 1	step 2	step 3	step 4

$$9\overline{)225} \quad\quad \begin{array}{r} 2 \\ 9\overline{)225} \\ \underline{18} \end{array} \quad\quad \begin{array}{r} 2 \\ 9\overline{)225} \\ \underline{18} \\ 4 \end{array} \quad\quad \begin{array}{r} 2 \\ 9\overline{)225} \\ \underline{18} \\ 45 \end{array} \quad\quad \begin{array}{r} 25 \\ 9\overline{)225} \\ \underline{18} \\ 45 \\ \underline{45} \\ r\,0 \end{array}$$

Here's the "formula" for the check step. 9 x 25 (+ r) = 225

Since r was 0 in this problem, 9 x 25 should equal 225. (Take a moment to multiply this out to make sure.)

Example 2:

step 1	step 2	step 3	step 4	step 5

$$\begin{array}{r} 4 \\ 7\overline{)307} \\ \underline{28} \end{array} \quad\quad \begin{array}{r} 4 \\ 7\overline{)307} \\ \underline{28} \\ 2 \end{array} \quad\quad \begin{array}{r} 4 \\ 7\overline{)307} \\ \underline{28} \\ 27 \end{array} \quad\quad \begin{array}{r} 43 \\ 7\overline{)307} \\ \underline{28} \\ 27 \\ \underline{21} \end{array} \quad\quad \begin{array}{r} 43 \\ 7\overline{)307} \\ \underline{28} \\ 27 \\ \underline{21} \\ r\,6 \end{array}$$

Check step.   7 x 43 (+ r) = 307

Since 7 x 43 is 301, and r is 6 ... 301 + 6 = 307.

So this problem checks as correct.

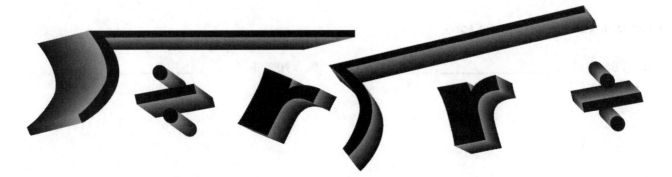

Name: _____ **Date:** _____

Dividing by Single-Digit Numbers (cont.) 8

 Solve the following division problems. Space has also been left for doing the check step for your answer.

1. $4 \overline{)404}$

2. $5 \overline{)650}$

3. $7 \overline{)810}$

check

check

check

4. $8 \overline{)704}$

5. $2 \overline{)673}$

6. $9 \overline{)599}$

check

check

check

Rewrite in vertical format and solve.

7. $786 \div 3 =$ _____

8. $900 \div 4 =$ _____

Understanding Factors: Dividing Made Easier 9

The factors of 16 are: 1, 2, 4, 8, 16.

This is because 1 • 16 = 16, 2 • 8 = 16, and 4 • 4 = 16.

✔ A **composite number**, such as 16, will have factors besides just 1 and itself.

✔ A **prime number** has only 1 and itself as factors. The numbers 11, 13, and 17 are examples of the many prime numbers.

Being able to recognize composite numbers or prime numbers is useful, not only for working with division, but also for working with fractions and equations. In a broad sense, factors allow problems to be separated into smaller, more easily managed pieces.

Factoring is easily accomplished by simply beginning at 2 and asking yourself "Is this number a factor?" (Since each number has 1 and itself as factors, it is not necessary to begin with 1.) Consider the following example.

Begin a list of factors ...

    20 :   1,   , 20

Is 2 a factor of 20 ? Yes, 2 x 10 = 20

Update the list of factors ...

    20 :   1, 2,   10, 20

Is 3 a factor of 20? No

Is 4 a factor of 20? Yes, 4 x 5 = 20

Update the list of factors ...

    20 :   1, 2, 4,   5, 10, 20

This is a complete list of the factors of 20. But how did we know to stop at 5? Since 5 x 5 is 25, checking larger numbers at this point will generate numbers larger than 20 and therefore not yield any new factors.

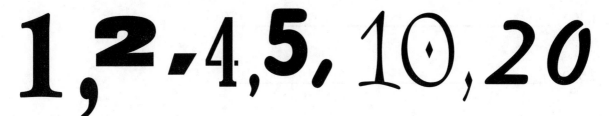

21

Name: _____   **Date:** _____

Understanding Factors: Dividing Made Easier (cont.) 9

APPLY!   List all factors for each number. Write "prime" if the number has only 1 and itself as factors.

1. 12 _____

2. 32 _____

3. 45 _____

4. 61 _____

5. 83 _____

6. 100 _____

7. 120 _____

For these larger numbers, name any two corresponding factors. (The purpose of this exercise is to recognize how numbers break down, not to spend a long time finding all of its factors.) The first one has been done for you.

500:    20 x 25   (Or 5 x 100 would have been another pair.)

8. 260: _____

9. 400: _____

10. 1,200: _____

11. 2,500: _____

Name: _____ **Date:** _____

Dividing by 10   **10**

 In previous sections, we worked with multiplying numbers by 10, 100, and 1,000. It was shown how a number such as 320 becomes 3,200 once it has been multiplied by 10.

Since division is the inverse operation of multiplication, it makes sense that numbers divided by 10 will be decreased in a similar fashion. The number that is divided by 10 should be reduced by one place value. Consider the following example.

$$900 \div 10 = 90$$

$$
\begin{array}{r} \\ 10\overline{)900} \end{array}
\qquad
\begin{array}{r} 9 \\ 10\overline{)900} \\ 90 \end{array}
\qquad
\begin{array}{r} 9 \\ 10\overline{)900} \\ \underline{90} \\ 00 \end{array}
\qquad
\begin{array}{r} 90 \\ 10\overline{)900} \\ \underline{90} \\ 000 \end{array}
$$

APPLY!

Solve by inspection.

1. $850 \div 10 =$ _____

2. $390 \div 10 =$ _____

3. $4{,}500 \div 10 =$ _____

4. $1{,}050 \div 10 =$ _____

5. $42{,}000 \div 10 =$ _____

6. $12{,}300 \div 10 =$ _____

Extension. Solve by inspection.

7. $3{,}000 \div 100 =$ _____

8. $50{,}000 \div 1{,}000 =$ _____

9. $1{,}200 \div 100 =$ _____

10. $8{,}800 \div 100 =$ _____

11. $15{,}000 \div 1{,}000 =$ _____

12. $25{,}500 \div 100 =$ _____

What Is r?

 We know that sometimes there is a **remainder** (r) left after a number has been divided. This remainder is actually a leftover portion that won't divide out "evenly." Consider the following solved problem:

$$
\begin{array}{r}
29 \\
7\overline{)207} \\
\underline{14} \\
67 \\
\underline{63} \\
r\,4
\end{array}
$$

In this example, 4 is the remainder. But what does that really mean?

This remainder is correctly written as a fraction $\frac{4}{7}$. In this problem:

$$207 \div 7 = 29\frac{4}{7}$$

And $29\frac{4}{7} \times 7 = 207$

The remainder is always a fraction, some amount less than one whole. A remainder is produced when the number being divided is not a multiple of the number it is being divided by.

$$7 \times 29 = 203$$

$$7 \times 30 = 210$$

207 is between 203 and 210.

So we can tell from this example why a remainder results from the division—7 is not a multiple of 207.

At this point, we'll write all of our remainders as fractions, since that's what they actually are. Don't worry at this point about reducing the fraction or trying to change it to a decimal equivalent.

Name: _____ **Date:** _____

What Is r? (cont.)

11

APPLY!

Solve each division problem. For those with remainders, write the remainder as a fraction.

1. 9)499   2. 5)7,811

    _____   _____

3. 8)625   4. 4)133

    _____   _____

5. 2)1,255   6. 6)555

    _____   _____

7. 3)378   8. 5)707

    _____   _____

Dividing by Two-Digit Numbers 12

 The process for dividing by two-digit numbers is almost identical to the process for dividing by single-digit numbers. Each portion of the number to be divided is considered in turn. The main difference is that working with a two-digit number means having to consider more digits in the number being divided. Consider the following problem.

$$25\overline{)368}$$

We begin this problem by looking at the first two digits of the number being divided and asking "Can 36 be divided by 25?" Since 36 is bigger than 25, the answer is "yes."

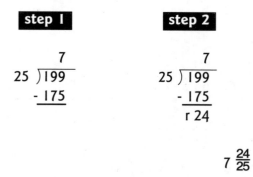

step 1	step 2	step 3	step 4

```
  step 1          step 2          step 3          step 4
     1               1              14              14
25 )368         25 )368         25 )368         25 )368
  - 25            - 25            - 25            - 25
                   118             118             118
                                 - 100           - 100
                                                  r 18
```

$$14\frac{18}{25}$$

In the example above, only the first two digits were needed in the first step. But what if the problem had been 199 ÷ 25? The first two digits "19" are not larger than 25. So the first three digits must be considered.

```
  step 1          step 2
      7               7
25 )199         25 )199
  - 175           - 175
                    r 24
```

$$7\frac{24}{25}$$

In this problem, we can see by inspection that 8 x 25 = 200, so it was expected that 7 with a "large" remainder would be the result. The number of steps in these kinds of problems depends on the size of the number being divided, but the process is the same regardless.

Name: _____ **Date:** _____

Dividing by Two-Digit Numbers (cont.) 12

APPLY!

Solve. For those with remainders, write the remainder as a fraction.

1. 13)615 _____

2. 40)388 _____

3. 75)642 _____

4. 31)999 _____

5. 90)6,155 _____

6. 15)3,250 _____

7. 28)26,624 _____

8. 67)60,750 _____

Name: _____ **Date:** _____

Dividing by Two-Digit Numbers (cont.) 12

9. $89 \overline{)16{,}800}$ _____ 10. $50 \overline{)50{,}000}$ _____

11. $10 \overline{)2{,}500}$ _____ 12. $48 \overline{)128{,}000}$ _____

13. Mr. Smith's relatives were saddened when the 103-year-old man died unexpectedly. After all expenses were paid, his estate was valued at $234,000. This amount will be split equally among his 52 surviving heirs. How much money will each heir receive?

    _____

14. A faulty computer at a factory caused 34,500 parts to be packaged incorrectly. If the parts can be re-packaged correctly by workers at a rate of 1,500 per day, how many days will it take to correct the error?

    _____

15. In a recent fundraiser for a charity, $4,340 was collected by 31 different volunteers. On average, how much money did each volunteer collect?

    _____

16. A herd of 1,680 cattle will be moved to 12 different pastures in order to keep the grass from being overgrazed in any one place. How many animals should go to each pasture to keep the numbers equal in each location?

    _____

Name: _____ Date: _____

Dividing by Three-Digit Numbers 13

The process for dividing by three-digit numbers is almost identical to the process for dividing by two-digit numbers. Each portion of the number to be divided is considered in turn. The main difference is that working with a three-digit number means having to consider more digits in the number being divided. Consider the following problem:

$$221 \overline{)4{,}850}$$

We begin this problem by looking at the first three digits of the number being divided and asking "Can 485 be divided by 221?" Since 485 is bigger than 221, the answer is "yes." (If 221 would not have gone into the first three digits, then we'd have been working with the first four digits in the initial step. This process is repeated for dividing by a three-digit number, or even if it's a ten-digit number.)

step 1	step 2	step 3	step 4

step 1
$$\begin{array}{r} 2 \\ 221 \overline{)4{,}850} \\ \underline{4\,42} \end{array}$$

step 2
$$\begin{array}{r} 2 \\ 221 \overline{)4{,}850} \\ \underline{-\,4\,42} \\ 430 \end{array}$$

step 3
$$\begin{array}{r} 21 \\ 221 \overline{)4{,}850} \\ \underline{4\,42} \\ 430 \\ -\,221 \end{array}$$

step 4
$$\begin{array}{r} 21 \\ 221 \overline{)4{,}850} \\ \underline{4\,42} \\ 430 \\ \underline{-221} \\ 209 \end{array}$$

$$21 \frac{209}{221}$$

APPLY!

Solve. For those with remainders, write the remainder as a fraction.

1. $125 \overline{)2{,}355}$ _____

2. $344 \overline{)1{,}299}$ _____

Name: _____ **Date:** _____

Dividing by Three-Digit Numbers (cont.) 13

3. $188 \overline{)2,090}$ _____

4. $900 \overline{)2,090}$ _____

5. $375 \overline{)13,750}$ _____

6. $100 \overline{)1,200}$ _____

7. $899 \overline{)1,100}$ _____

8. $641 \overline{)18,822}$ _____

9. $705 \overline{)205,800}$ _____

10. $615 \overline{)972,803}$ _____

Name: _____ **Date:** _____

Section Review 2

APPLY!

Solve.

1.	388 x 7	**2.**	819 x 11	**3.**	1,275 x 50	
4.	1,606 x 64	**5.**	7,800 x 125	**6.**	12,240 x 10	
7.	50,500 x 100	**8.**	98,000 x 36	**9.**	44,520 x 240	

List all factors for each of the numbers given. Write "prime" if the number has only itself and 1 as factors.

10. 24 _____

11. 38 _____

12. 50 _____

Name: _____ **Date:** _____

Section Review 2 (cont.)

Solve. For those with remainders, write the remainder as a fraction.

13. $7 \overline{)225}$

14. $3 \overline{)188}$

15. $15 \overline{)495}$

_____   _____   _____

16. $68 \overline{)8,688}$

17. $75 \overline{)7,500}$

18. $125 \overline{)4,625}$

_____   _____   _____

19. $100 \overline{)12,000}$

20. $359 \overline{)22,435}$

21. $725 \overline{)80,561}$

_____   _____   _____

A Quick Look at Decimal Numbers **14**

(A calculator is recommended for this activity.)

 In previous sections, we divided numbers, and sometimes a remainder was produced. These remainders are leftover portions after the division has taken place. We learned that remainders can be written as a fraction, as shown in the following example.

$$36 \frac{16}{28}$$
$$28 \overline{)1,024}$$

In this solved problem, $36 \frac{16}{28}$ was found to be the answer. But $36 \frac{16}{28}$ is a whole number with a fractional portion. Fractions are appropriate in mathematics, but they are seldom used in banking or at the supermarket, for example. Try working the following problem on your calculator:

$$1,024 \div 28 = ?$$

$$1,024 \div 28 = 36.571428 \quad \text{(This is what your calculator}$$
should show—a bit different
from $36 \frac{16}{28}$ isn't it?)

Actually, these numbers 36.571428 and $36 \frac{16}{28}$ mean almost the same thing.

$\frac{16}{28}$ actually means $16 \div 28$

On your calculator, try $16 \div 28 = ?$

(You'll get 0.5714285)

What does this mean? A number with a fraction, such as $4\frac{3}{4}$, can be thought of as:

$$4\frac{3}{4} = 4 + \frac{3}{4} = 4 + (3 \div 4) = 4 + (0.75) = 4.75$$

To convert a fraction to a decimal number, the formula is:

> **top number ÷ bottom number = decimal equivalent**

The calculator sometimes gives an exact answer, but sometimes the fraction cannot be expressed in the number of spaces available on the calculator's screen. So it's ordinarily sufficient to express answers to four places beyond the decimal, since digits past the fourth decimal place tend to represent very small numbers.

Name: _____ Date: _____

A Quick Look at Decimal Numbers (cont.) 14

APPLY! Using a calculator, convert the whole numbers with fractional portions to decimal numbers. Express answers only to four places after the decimal.

1. $3\frac{3}{8}$ = 3. _____

2. $10\frac{16}{19}$ = 10. _____

3. $24\frac{34}{109}$ = 24. _____

4. $59\frac{1}{9}$ = 59. _____

5. $164\frac{202}{239}$ = 164. _____

6. $185\frac{17}{40}$ = 185. _____

7. $44\frac{9}{50}$ = 44. _____

8. $16\frac{7}{8}$ = 16. _____

9. $194\frac{34}{40}$ = 194. _____

10. $5\frac{663}{665}$ = 5. _____

Calculator Practice. Solve.

11. 240 x 88.5 = _____

12. 4.25 x 100 = _____

13. 1,000 x 1.1 = _____

14. 1,800 x 50.33 = _____

15. 4,200 ÷ 12.6 = _____

16. 18,000 x 0.88 = _____

17. 12,002 ÷ 240 = _____

18. 60 ÷ 1.5 = _____

19. 742 ÷ 8.07 = _____

20. 95 ÷ 7 = _____

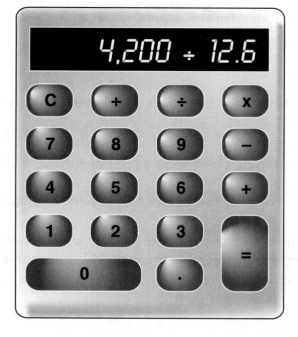

Multiplying With Decimal Numbers **15**

Except for the final step, multiplying with decimal numbers represents the same process as with whole numbers. Consider the following solved problems.

Example 1

```
     1240
   x 10.5
     6200
    00000
 + 124000
   130200
```
(This is the step where the decimal must be accounted for.)

Go back to the original problem and note how many places are to the right of the decimal. The "5" is the only digit to the right of the decimal. Now turn your attention to the answer "130200." To finish the problem, we account for the decimal by counting one place to the left. Our answer becomes 13,020.0, or more simply written, 13,020.

Example 2

```
     1618
   x 1.44
     6472
    64720
 + 161800
   232992
```

After counting over 2 decimal places to account for the two digits to the right of the decimal (.44) in the original problem, we have an answer:

2,329.92

If decimals appear in both numbers being multiplied, the total number of digits to the right of the decimal is counted, and that total is used for correctly placing the decimal point in the answer.

35

Name: _____ **Date:** _____

Multiplying With Decimal Numbers (cont.) 15

APPLY!

Solve.

I.	180 x 2.2	**2.**	669 x 10.3	**3.**	1,450 x 4.55

I.   180
      x 2.2

2.   669
      x 10.3

3.   1,450
      x 4.55

4.   2,500
      x 2.44

5.   7,422
      x 1.8

6.   12,800
      x 0.425

7.   100.2
      x 80

8.   340.88
      x 2.6

9.   15.75
      x 40

Dividing With Decimal Numbers 16

We saw in previous work with multiplying decimal numbers that the final step in the problem is determining where the decimal is placed. Division is a bit different, since the decimal must be the first thing considered. If the divisor is a decimal number, it must first be made into a whole number by moving the decimal. Consider the problem below and how it changes.

Example 1

$7.5 \overline{)225}$ becomes $75. \overline{)2250.}$ (The divisor, 75, is now a whole number.)

In this problem, the decimal has been shifted one place to the right in order to make the divisor a whole number. Likewise, the number being divided has also had its decimal shifted one place to the right, the same effect as multiplying it by 10. Consider the next problem.

Example 2

step 1 (Make divisor a whole number.)

$2.25 \overline{)474.75}$ becomes $225. \overline{)47475.}$ (It's the same as multiplying both numbers by 100.)

Now it's the same as solving any division problem:

step 2	step 3	step 4	step 5

```
     2              21             211            211
225 )47475      225 )47475      225 )47475     225 )47475
   - 450           - 450          - 450          - 450
                     247            247            247
                     225            225            225
                                    225            225
                                    225            225
                                                  r 0
```

How can a decimal just be moved to make the divisor a whole number? It is okay, since the number being divided is changed by the same amount, preserving the relationship between the two numbers.

23.5 ÷ 1.492 ÷ 83.7 ÷ 16.9

37

Name: _____ **Date:** _____

Dividing With Decimal Numbers (cont.) 16

Solve by first making the divisor a whole number.

I. $5.5 \overline{)396}$

2. $4.8 \overline{)196.8}$

3. $3.2 \overline{)345.6}$

4. $1.25 \overline{)77.5}$

5. $10.8 \overline{)950.4}$

6. $6.45 \overline{)483.75}$

7. $22.6 \overline{)406.8}$

8. $20.25 \overline{)810}$

9. $14.88 \overline{)2,023.68}$

10. $22,033.2 \div 120.4 =$ _____

Estimating the Result of Multiplication and Division 17

 There are many circumstances where having a quick estimate of the result of multiplication or division is preferable to taking the time to get an exact answer. Sometimes estimates even turn out to be very close to the actual answer.

Example 1:

3,281 people attend a concert, paying $9.69 per ticket.

What would be a fast way to find out about how much money was collected at the concert?

Think ... about 3,300 people times about $10 per ticket.
Result ... about $33,000 was taken in.

The actual amount would have been $31,792.89. We can see that our estimate was a little high because we rounded 3,281 up to 3,300 and the ticket price $9.69 up to an even $10. So we would have expected our estimate to be just a bit high.

Example 2:

 7,500 apples are to be packed in boxes that will hold about 40 apples each.

What would be a fast estimate for about how many boxes of apples will be produced, once all of the apples are packed?

Think ... Recognize that 8,000 would be a multiple of 40.
Result ... will be slightly less than 200 boxes.

The actual amount would be 187.5 boxes of apples. We expected the number to be near, but not quite 200, since we rounded 7,500 up to 8,000 for the division.

Example 3:

211 T-shirts screenprinted per hour for 8 hours, 45 minutes.

About how many shirts were produced all total? (In this example, we'll rely on our estimate instead of getting an exact answer in the last step.)

Think ... about 200 shirts per hour for nearly 9 hours
Result ... about 1,800 shirts printed

Name: _____ **Date:** _____

Estimating the Result of Multiplication and Division (cont.) 17

APPLY! For each situation described, provide the Think and Result steps. Since this activity relies on estimation, it is possible to arrive at different answers, depending on the numbers you choose for the Think step.

1. Total weight of 414 salmon caught in a net with most fish weighing in the 5-pound range.

   Think _____

   Result _____

2. Number of pieces of clay that may be taken from a 110-pound lump of clay, if each piece taken is about 4 pounds.

   Think _____

   Result _____

3. Amount of toll collected in one toll booth where 5,787 cars and trucks passed through, each paying a toll of $0.45.

   Think _____

   Result _____

4. Total number of letters delivered by a postal carrier on a busy day, if she visited 407 houses with each house receiving an average of nine pieces of mail.

   Think _____

   Result _____

5. There is a sales force of 10 salespeople at a company that serves 1,155 customers. About how many customers should each salesperson be assigned?

   Think _____

   Result _____

Name: _____ **Date:** _____

Final Review: All Sections

1. Use the model shown below to demonstrate the division problem:

   $43 \div 6 = 7 \, r1$

   ★ ★ ★ ★ ★ ★ ★ ★ ★ ★
   ★ ★ ★ ★ ★ ★ ★ ★ ★ ★
   ★ ★ ★ ★ ★ ★ ★ ★ ★ ★
   ★ ★ ★ ★ ★ ★ ★ ★ ★ ★
   ★ ★ ★

For each of the numbers given, provide the next eight multiples.

2. 8 _____

3. 20 _____

4. 110 _____

5. 250 _____

List all factors for each of the numbers. Write "prime" if the number has only 1 and itself as factors.

6. 17 _____

7. 27 _____

8. 39 _____

9. 64 _____

Name: _____ **Date:** _____

Final Review: All Topics (cont.)

10.   335
       x   6

11.   117
       x   9

12.   599
       x 10

13.   1,230
       x   10

14.   850
       x 12

15.   729
       x 42

16.   42,200
     x   88

17.   375
       x 100

18.   11,600
     x   325

19. Five trucks have been loaded with building materials for a job site. Each truck is carrying 12,020 pounds of wallboard. How many pounds of wallboard will have been delivered, once these five trucks leave their loads at the job site?

_____

20. Water passes through a particular pipe at the water treatment facility at a rate of 80 gallons per minute when flowing at full capacity. How many gallons of water per hour can pass through this pipe?

_____

Name: _____ **Date:** _____

Final Review: All Topics (cont.)

21. $7\overline{)749}$

22. $8\overline{)1,200}$

23. $10\overline{)5,000}$

Write remainders as a fraction.

24. $55\overline{)15,000}$

25. $120\overline{)20,000}$

26. $432\overline{)44,880}$

Mixed practice with decimal numbers. Solve.

27.
$$\begin{array}{r} 1,482 \\ \times\ \ 8.2 \\ \hline \end{array}$$

28.
$$\begin{array}{r} 5,600 \\ \times\ \ 10.5 \\ \hline \end{array}$$

29. $4.4\overline{)240}$

Short answer.

30. Why is it sometimes more reasonable to use estimation for solving multiplication or division problems than providing an exact answer?

_____

_____

_____

Answer Keys

What Are Multiplication and Division? (pages 4–5)

1. 3, 8, 24   **2.** 4, 4, 16   **3.** 7, 6, 42   **4.** 2, 12, 24   **5.** 9, 4, 36
6. Answers will vary.

Math Facts: Multiplication Tables and Multiples (pages 6–7)

1. 6, 12, 18, 24, 30, 36, 42, 48, 54, 60, 66, 72
2. 4, 8, 12, 16, 20, 24, 28, 32, 36, 40, 44, 48
3. 10, 20, 30, 40, 50, 60, 70, 80, 90, 100, 110, 120
4. 7, 14, 21, 28, 35, 42, 49, 56, 63, 70, 77, 84
5. 18   **6.** 99   **7.** 21   **8.** 110   **9.** 30   **10.** 40   **11.** 32   **12.** 36   **13.** 12
14. 55   **15.** 16   **16.** 24   **17.** 45   **18.** 30   **19.** 42   **20.** 9   **21.** 44   **22.** 56
23. 27   **24.** 28   **25.** 81   **26.** 77   **27.** 16   **28.** 54   **29.** 60   **30.** 132

Multiplying by a Single-Digit Number (page 9)

1. 669   **2.** 228   **3.** 969   **4.** 1,676   **5.** 3,380   **6.** 1,824
7. 3,708   **8.** 1,794   **9.** 6,939   **10.** 3,605   **11.** 747   **12.** 2,536
13. 8,991   **14.** 707   **15.** 4,220   **16.** 3,184   **17.** 2,832

The Easy Process of Multiplying by 10 (page 10)

1. 750   **2.** 1,450   **3.** 9,000   **4.** 22,400   **5.** 3,130   **6.** 5,550
7. 10,000   **8.** 1,020   **9.** 120,050   **10.** 8,500

Multiplying by Two-Digit Numbers (page 12)

1. 5,313   **2.** 4,444   **3.** 5,124   **4.** 8,180   **5.** 51,870   **6.** 27,166
7. 16,800   **8.** 388,875   **9.** 115,500   **10.** 84,450   **11.** 25,245   **12.** 2,239,872

Multiplying by Three-Digit Numbers (pages 13–14)

1. 28,408   **2.** 15,561   **3.** 224,775   **4.** 115,620   **5.** 702,119   **6.** 1,606,500
7. 300,625   **8.** 2,000,000   **9.** 936,775   **10.** 309,465   **11.** 1,308,000   **12.** 24,150,000

Multiplying by 100, 1,000, or More (page 15)

1. 7,500   **2.** 340   **3.** 25,500   **4.** 51,500   **5.** 885,000   **6.** 1,542,000
7. 451,000   **8.** 650,000   **9.** 3,750,000   **10.** 10,000,000

Section Review 1 (pages 16–17)

1. 3, 6, 9, 12, 15, 18, 21, 24, 27   **2.** 11, 22, 33, 44, 55, 66, 77, 88, 99
3. 15, 30, 45, 60, 75, 90, 105, 120, 135   **4.** 25, 50, 75, 100, 125, 150, 175, 200, 225
5. 405   **6.** 1,380   **7.** 10,625   **8.** 1,463   **9.** 13,950   **10.** 15,500
11. 25,125   **12.** 2,500   **13.** $5,700   **14.** 980   **15.** 85,000   **16.** 18,260 lbs.
17. 92,900   **18.** 388,010   **19.** 239,200   **20.** 1,875,000   **21.** 200,000
22. 7,860,000

Dividing by Single-Digit Numbers (page 20)
1. 101 2. 130 3. 115 r5 4. 88 5. 336 r1 6. 66 r5
7. 262 8. 225

Understanding Factors: Dividing Made Easier (page 22)
1. 1, 2, 3, 4, 6, 12 2. 1, 2, 4, 8, 16, 32 3. 1, 3, 5, 9, 15, 45 4. prime
5. prime 6. 1, 2, 4, 5, 10, 20, 25, 50, 100
7. 1, 2, 3, 4, 5, 6, 8, 10, 12, 15, 20, 24, 30, 40, 60, 120 8–11. Answers will vary.

Dividing by 10 (page 23)
1. 85 2. 39 3. 450 4. 105 5. 4,200 6. 1,230
7. 30 8. 50 9. 12 10. 88 11. 15 12. 255

What Is r? (page 25)
1. $55\frac{4}{9}$ 2. $1,562\frac{1}{5}$ 3. $78\frac{1}{8}$ 4. $33\frac{1}{4}$ 5. $627\frac{1}{2}$ 6. $92\frac{3}{6}$
7. 126 8. $141\frac{2}{5}$

Dividing by Two-Digit Numbers (pages 27–28)
1. $47\frac{4}{13}$ 2. $9\frac{28}{40}$ 3. $8\frac{42}{75}$ 4. $32\frac{7}{31}$ 5. $68\frac{35}{90}$ 6. $216\frac{10}{15}$
7. $950\frac{24}{28}$ 8. $906\frac{48}{67}$ 9. $188\frac{68}{89}$ 10. 1,000 11. 250 12. $2,666\frac{32}{48}$
13. \$4,500 14. 23 15. \$140 16. 140

Dividing by Three-Digit Numbers (pages 29–30)
1. $18\frac{105}{125}$ 2. $3\frac{267}{344}$ 3. $11\frac{22}{188}$ 4. $2\frac{290}{900}$ 5. $36\frac{250}{375}$ 6. 12
7. $1\frac{201}{899}$ 8. $29\frac{233}{641}$ 9. $291\frac{645}{705}$ 10. $1,581\frac{488}{615}$

Section Review 2 (pages 31–32)
1. 2,716 2. 9,009 3. 63,750 4. 102,784 5. 975,000 6. 122,400
7. 5,050,000 8. 3,528,000 9. 10,684,800 10. 1, 2, 3, 4, 6, 8, 12, 24
11. 1, 2, 19, 38 12. 1, 2, 5, 10, 25, 50 13. $32\frac{1}{7}$ 14. $62\frac{2}{3}$ 15. 33
16. $127\frac{52}{68}$ 17. 100 18. 37 19. 120 20. $62\frac{177}{359}$ 21. $111\frac{86}{725}$

A Quick Look at Decimal Numbers (page 34)
1. .375 2. .8421 3. .3119 4. .1111 5. .8451 6. .425
7. .18 8. .875 9. .85 10. .9969 11. 21,240 12. 425
13. 1,100 14. 90,594 15. 333.3333 16. 15,840 17. 50.0083 18. 40
19. 91.9454 20. 13.5714

Multiplying With Decimal Numbers (page 36)
1. 396 2. 6,890.7 3. 6,597.50 4. 6,100 5. 13,359.6 6. 5,440
7. 8,016 8. 886.288 9. 630

Dividing With Decimal Numbers (page 38)

1. 72	**2.** 41	**3.** 108	**4.** 62	**5.** 88	**6.** 75
7. 18	**8.** 40	**9.** 136	**10.** 183		

Estimating the Result of Multiplication and Division (page 40)
Answers will vary.

Final Review: All Sections (pages 41–43)

1. 7 groups of 6 should be circled, with 1 star left uncircled
2. 8, 16, 24, 32, 40, 48, 56, 64, 72
3. 20, 40, 60, 80, 100, 120, 140, 160, 180
4. 110, 220, 330, 440, 550, 660, 770, 880, 990
5. 250; 500; 750; 1,000; 1,250; 1,500; 1,750; 2,000; 2,250

6. prime	**7.** 1, 3, 9, 27	**8.** 1, 3, 13, 39	**9.** 1, 2, 4, 8, 16, 32, 64
10. 2,010	**11.** 1,053	**12.** 5,990	**13.** 12,300
14. 10,200	**15.** 30,618	**16.** 3,713,600	**17.** 37,500
18. 3,770,000	**19.** 60,100	**20.** 4,800	**21.** 107
22. 150	**23.** 500	**24.** $272\frac{40}{55}$	**25.** $166\frac{80}{120}$
26. $103\frac{384}{432}$	**27.** 12,152.4	**28.** 58,800	**29.** 54.54
30. Answers will vary.			